Night Sky

Written by Janine Amos
Designed by Claire Brisley and Cath Adsett
Reading consultants: Christopher Collier and Alan Howe,
Bath Spa University, UK Bath Spa University, UK

This edition published by Parragon in 2011

Parragon
Queen Street House
4 Queen Street
Bath BA1 1HE, UK

ISBN 978-1-4454-4660-8

Printed in China

DISCOVERY KIDS™
Night Sky

PaRRagon

Bath · New York · Singapore · Hong Kong · Cologne · Delhi
Melbourne · Amsterdam · Johannesburg · Auckland · Shenzhen

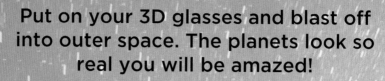

Put on your 3D glasses and blast off into outer space. The planets look so real you will be amazed!

Parents' notes

This book is part of a series of non-fiction books designed to appeal to children learning to read.

Each book has been developed with the help of educational experts.

At the end of the book is a quiz to help your child remember the information and the meanings of some of the words and sentences. Difficult words, which appear in bold in the book, can be found in the glossary at the back. There is also an index.

Contents

Night sky

When you look at the night sky you can see thousands of stars. They are so far away that they look tiny. But really they are giant balls of glowing gas.

The Sun

All the stars we can see are part of our **galaxy**. A galaxy is a massive group of stars. Our Sun is a star.

The Milky Way

There are a lot of galaxies in the universe. Our galaxy is called the Milky Way.

DISCOVERY FACT™

The temperature at the heart of a star reaches around 29 million degrees Fahrenheit.

Our star

The Sun is our closest star. It is over a million times bigger than Earth.

Earth and the other **planets** travel around the Sun along paths called orbits. As they go, they spin around and around like tops. They are kept in their orbit by a force called **gravity**.

It takes Earth about 365 days, or one year, to orbit the Sun.

The Moon orbits Earth. This takes about one month.

Earth's orbit

DISCOVERY FACT™

The center of the Sun is like a massive bomb—it is always exploding!

The planets

All the **planets** that orbit the Sun are different. On some the air is poisonous. Others are burning hot, or freezing cold, or covered in dust.

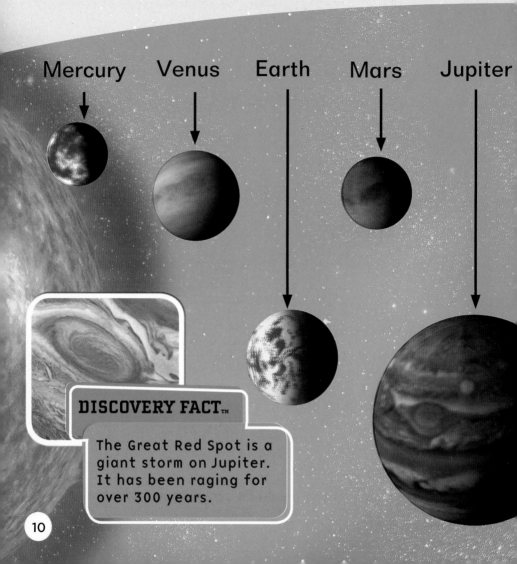

Mercury   Venus   Earth   Mars   Jupiter

DISCOVERY FACT™

The Great Red Spot is a giant storm on Jupiter. It has been raging for over 300 years.

The four planets closest to the Sun are called inner planets. They are made mainly of rock and metal. Earth is one of them.

The planets farthest from the Sun are called outer planets. They are huge balls made mainly of gas.

Neptune

Saturn

Uranus

Other space objects

Have you ever seen a shooting star streaking across the night sky? **Space** is not completely empty. There is dust, gas, rock, and ice flying around at high speed.

Asteroids are massive space rocks. Most move around the Sun in a band called the asteroid belt.

Comets are balls of ice with long, shining tails of dust and gas.

A comet

A meteor

Meteors are made of burning space dust. We know them as "shooting stars."

Every year, thousands of space rocks fall onto Earth. Most fall into the ocean.

DISCOVERY FACT™

This crater is in Arizona. It was made by a meteor crashing into Earth about 50,000 years ago.

Our solar system

The **planets** and their moons are part of our **solar system**. So is everything else that travels around the Sun, from the largest asteroid to the smallest speck of dust.

Sun

Mercury

Earth

Saturn

Uranu

Our solar system also contains at least four dwarf planets. Eris is the biggest dwarf planet.

Venus

Mars

Jupiter

Neptune

Cerro Tololo Observatory in Chile

DISCOVERY FACT™

In 1957, Sputnik 1 was the first **satellite** to be launched into orbit by a rocket. It was about 23 inches across.

Looking into space

For hundreds of years people have used telescopes to look into **space**. Telescopes make faraway objects look closer.

Big telescopes are kept in buildings called observatories. Observatories are built on high land away from city lights.

Earth's **atmosphere** stops us from seeing some stars and **planets**. The Hubble Space Telescope orbits beyond the atmosphere so it can see more clearly into space.

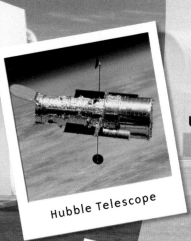

Hubble Telescope

Satellite dishes

A satellite dish collects radio waves given off by objects in space. In New Mexico, lots of dishes work together.

Famous astronomers

People have been studying the universe for thousands of years. People who study **space** are called astronomers.

Galileo Galilei (1564–1642) was one of the first people to use a telescope to study the sky. He learned that the **planets** move around the Sun.

Isaac Newton (1643–1727) figured out why the planets move around the Sun. He learned that a force called **gravity** keeps them circling there.

Johannes Kepler (1571–1630) used mathematics to figure out how the planets move.

William Herschel (1738–1822) built a huge telescope. His sister was also an astronomer.

When astronauts work outside, they wear a special suit to protect them.

Astronauts in space

Hundreds of people have traveled into **space**. Maybe one day you might travel into space, too.

Yuri Gagarin was the first person in space. He was a Russian **cosmonaut**. He traveled once around Earth.

Neil Armstrong, an American **astronaut**, was the first person to walk on the Moon. His footprint is still there. There is no rain and no wind to blow it away.

Yuri Gagarin

Neil Armstrong

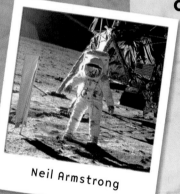

DISCOVERY FACT™

In 1957, a Russian dog named Laika was the first animal to be sent into space.

Space station

A space station is a huge workplace in **space**. People carry out experiments there, and collect information about the stars and **planets**.

The International Space Station

There is **microgravity** in space. It makes you feel as if you are floating. Objects will float about, too. Everything in the space station is strapped down.

Crew members attach their sleeping bags to the station's walls for a good night's sleep.

Sleeping in space

Eating in space

DISCOVERY FACT™

Which way is up? **Astronauts** attach themselves to their workstations with Velcro.

Voyagers I and II are traveling in deep **space**. They carry friendly messages in case aliens find them.

Space probes

Robot **probes** explore places people cannot reach, and send information back to Earth.

Galileo space probe

The probe Galileo traveled around Jupiter 34 times. It sent pictures and information back to Earth.

Cassini-Huygens

The Cassini-Huygens spacecraft reached Saturn and its moons in 2004. The Huygens probe can collect far more information than a human space explorer.

DISCOVERY FACT™

Two thirds of probes sent to Mars have not completed their missions. It's called the Mars Curse!

Quiz

Now try this quiz!
All the answers can be
found in this book.

What is our galaxy called?

a) The Donut

b) The Chocolate Cake

c) The Milky Way

Which was the first
animal to be
sent into space?

a) A dog

b) A cat

c) A horse

Where do you put your
sleeping bag in a space
station?

a) In a tent

b) On the floor

c) On the wall

Acknowledgements

t=top, c=center, b=bottom, r=right, l=left

Cover: iStockphoto

p.1 Time & Life Pictures/Getty Image, p.4-5 V Piskunov/ iStockphoto, p.6 Alessandro Della Bella/epa/Corbis, p6-7 D Marinov, p.8-9 Denis Scott/Corbis/E Terentev/iStockphoto, p9.c Denis Scott/Corbis, p.9bl Farhad Parsa/zefa/Corbis, p.10 Tim Kiusalaas/Corbis, p.10bl PhotoLink/Getty, p.11 Tim Kiusalaas/ Corbis, p.12-13 Denis Scott/CorbisJames, p.12c Roger Ressmeyer/ Corbis, p.12b Reuters/Corbis, p.14-15 Denis Scott/Corbis, p.14 -15 Tim Kiusalaas/Corbis, p.16b Harry Frank/iStockphoto, p.16-17 Mark Chivers/Robert Harding World Imagery/Corbis, p.17t NASA, p.17b Richard T. Nowitz/Corbis, p.18l Bettmann/Corbis, p.19tr The Gallery Collection/Corbis, p.19ml Rune Hellestad/Corbis, p.19bl Bettmann/Corbis, p.19br Bettmann/Corbis, p.20-21 Corbis, p.21t Bettmann/Corbis, p.21c Bettmann/Corbis, p.21b Marc Garanger/ Corbis, p.22-23c NASA via CNP, p.23br NASA, p.23tl NASA, p.23tr NASA, p.23bl NASA, p.24-25 Time & Life Pictures/Getty Image, p.25c epa/Corbis, p.25tr NASA/JSC, p.25c epa/Corbis, p.25b epa/Corbis, p.26-27 Bryan Allen/Corbis

Stickers: additional images supplied by Corbis and NASA